TOULOUSE
TRAVEL
GUIDE

Discovering the Rich Heritage, Gastronomic Delights, and Hidden Gems of Toulouse"

JACKSON COLE

TABLE OF CONTENT

INTRODUCTION

Toulouse, the captivating Pink City of southwestern France, holds a special place in my heart as one of the most enchanting destinations I have ever visited. Its rich history, vibrant culture, and warm hospitality made my trip an unforgettable experience.

As I arrived in Toulouse, the first thing that struck me was the city's distinctive pink hue, visible on many of its historical buildings. The Basilica of Saint-Sernin, an impressive Romanesque structure, welcomed me with open arms, offering a glimpse into the city's medieval past. I marveled at the intricate architecture and the serene atmosphere within its walls, feeling a deep sense of reverence for the history that unfolded here.

Another highlight of my trip was exploring the charming Capitole de Toulouse, the city's town hall located in the heart of the bustling main square.

The grand facade and the bustling activity around it were mesmerizing. Inside, the ornate halls showcased Toulouse's proud heritage, and I couldn't help but feel humbled to be standing at the center of such rich cultural significance.

One of my favorite experiences was strolling through the picturesque Jardin des Plantes. The beautifully landscaped gardens, adorned with vibrant flowers and tranquil ponds, offered a perfect escape from the city's hustle and bustle. As I sat under the shade of a tree, I savored the peacefulness and reflected on the beauty of nature intertwined with urban life.

Toulouse's art and museums left a lasting impression on me as well. The Musée des Augustins displayed a remarkable collection of artworks from various periods, including impressive sculptures and striking paintings. It was a journey through time, a glimpse into the creative minds that have shaped the city's artistic landscape.

Delving into the local cuisine was an absolute delight. I savored the flavors of traditional Toulousain dishes, especially the iconic Cassoulet. The rich combination of beans, sausages, and tender meats was a true gastronomic indulgence that left me craving for more.

As I explored beyond the city limits, I embarked on day trips to neighboring towns and picturesque landscapes. The medieval fortifications of Carcassonne and the serene beauty of the Canal du Midi were nothing short of magical. These excursions offered a perfect balance between historical immersion and natural wonders.

Yet, it was the hidden gems of Toulouse that truly stole my heart. Exploring lesser-known neighborhoods and stumbling upon quirky boutiques and craft shops added a sense of intrigue and discovery to my journey. The city's locals were warm, welcoming, and always willing to share stories about their beloved home, which made my experience even more authentic and heartfelt.

My trip to Toulouse coincided with the vibrant Violet Festival, and I was fortunate enough to participate in the festivities. The city came alive with colors, music, and laughter as locals and tourists alike celebrated the flower that symbolizes Toulouse. The atmosphere was infectious, leaving me with memories of dancing in the streets and forging new friendships with people from all walks of life.

As my time in Toulouse drew to a close, I found myself filled with a mix of emotions—gratitude for the wonderful experiences, a tinge of sadness to bid adieu to this captivating city, and excitement at the prospect of returning someday. Toulouse had woven its magic around me, leaving an indelible mark on my heart.

In conclusion, my memorable experience in Toulouse was a beautiful tapestry of history, culture, and warmth. The Pink City's allure, its hidden treasures, and the genuine hospitality of its people made it a journey that I will cherish for a lifetime. Toulouse is not just a destination; it's a soul-stirring experience that has forever become a part of who I am.

Welcome to the Pink City

Nestled in the picturesque landscape of southwestern France, Toulouse is an enchanting city that beckons travelers with its distinctive charm and warm ambiance. Known as the "Pink City" due to the rosy hues of its historical buildings, this destination exudes a unique allure that captivates the heart and soul of every visitor.

Stepping foot into Toulouse, you'll be instantly enveloped by its rich history dating back to ancient Roman times. The Basilica of Saint-Sernin, an architectural masterpiece and a UNESCO World Heritage site, stands as a testament to the city's medieval legacy. As you walk through the cobblestone streets, you'll discover an intriguing blend of old-world charm and modern vibrancy.

The beating heart of Toulouse lies in its bustling main square, home to the majestic Capitole de Toulouse. The grand facade of this town hall dominates the square, offering a majestic welcome to all who enter. From here, the city's lively atmosphere unfolds, with vibrant cafes, charming boutiques, and street performers adding a touch of liveliness to the surroundings.

But it's not just the impressive landmarks that make Toulouse special; it's the inviting ambiance that envelops you like a warm embrace. The locals, known for their warm hospitality, welcome visitors with open arms, eager to share the city's hidden treasures and cherished traditions. Engaging in conversations with the Toulousains opens up a world of insights into the city's cultural heritage and local way of life.

Toulouse is a haven for art and culture enthusiasts. The city's museums house an impressive collection of artworks, showcasing the talents of both past and present generations. From classical masterpieces to contemporary exhibits, the art scene in Toulouse is diverse and ever-evolving, providing a treat for the creative senses.

As dusk falls, Toulouse comes alive with its vibrant nightlife. The city's bars, clubs, and entertainment venues offer something for every taste, creating an electrifying atmosphere that promises unforgettable evenings filled with laughter and joy.

When it comes to gastronomy, Toulouse is a true culinary paradise. The region's renowned dishes, such as the iconic Cassoulet, are a celebration of flavors and traditional savoir-faire. Exploring the local food markets, indulging in gourmet restaurants, and savoring the finest wines will be a culinary journey like no other.

Beyond the city's boundaries, Toulouse's natural surroundings enchant with their beauty. From the peaceful Jardin des Plantes to the majestic Pyrenees Mountains, outdoor enthusiasts will find endless opportunities for adventure and relaxation.

Welcome to the Pink City, where history, culture, and modernity intertwine to create an experience that will stay with you forever. Whether you are here to explore its heritage, indulge in its culinary delights, or simply bask in the warmth of its ambiance, Toulouse promises a journey that will leave you enchanted and inspired. So, immerse yourself in the colors, flavors, and rhythms of the Pink City, and let Toulouse work its magic on your soul.

Brief History of Toulouse

Toulouse, the Pink City of southwestern France, boasts a history that stretches back over two millennia, making it one of the country's oldest and most significant cities. The city's origins can be traced to an ancient settlement established by the Celtic Volcae Tectosages in the 4th century BCE. This early Celtic presence laid the foundation for Toulouse's cultural and historical tapestry.

During the Roman era, Toulouse, then known as "Tolosa," became a vital hub for trade and commerce. It was strategically positioned along the Roman road linking Bordeaux to Narbonne, facilitating the movement of goods across the region. The Romans left a lasting imprint on the city's infrastructure, and remnants of their influence can still be seen in some of Toulouse's architectural wonders, such as the Basilica of Saint-Sernin.

Over the centuries, Toulouse witnessed various shifts in power and dominion. In the 5th century CE, the Visigoths captured the city, followed by the Franks in the 6th century, who incorporated it into the Frankish Empire. The medieval period saw Toulouse flourish as a center of learning, art, and spirituality, exemplified by the construction of magnificent structures like the Basilica of Saint-Sernin, a testament to the city's religious importance.

Toulouse played a crucial role in the Albigensian Crusade during the 13th century. The city's association with the Cathars, a religious sect considered heretical by the Catholic Church, led to a brutal conflict known as the Albigensian Crusade. After a lengthy siege, Toulouse finally surrendered to the French Crown in 1229, marking the end of its independence.

The Renaissance era witnessed Toulouse's revival as a cultural and intellectual center. Renowned thinkers and artists graced its streets, contributing to the city's cultural effervescence. However, the religious wars that followed, particularly during the 16th century, brought periods of turbulence and strife to Toulouse.

In the subsequent centuries, Toulouse grew as a hub for the aerospace industry. The establishment of Airbus in the 20th century significantly boosted the city's economy and solidified its position as a key player in the global aviation industry. Today, Toulouse is known as "Aerospace Valley" due to the presence of major aerospace companies and research institutions.

Throughout its long history, Toulouse has preserved its cultural heritage and unique identity. The blending of Celtic, Roman, Gothic, and Renaissance influences has given rise to a captivating cityscape that captivates visitors from around the world. Its pink-tinted facades, medieval streets, and vibrant cultural scene offer a glimpse into the layers of history that have shaped Toulouse into the extraordinary destination it is today.

As Toulouse continues to evolve, it remains a testament to the resilience of its people, who have nurtured their city's heritage while embracing progress and innovation. Each corner of Toulouse tells a story, and its history lives on in the hearts of its inhabitants and the memories of all who walk its streets.

Getting to Know the Local Culture

Exploring Toulouse goes beyond admiring its architectural marvels and indulging in its culinary delights. To truly embrace the spirit of the Pink City, getting to know its local culture is a must. The warm and vibrant culture of Toulouse is deeply rooted in its history, traditions, and the genuine hospitality of its people.

One of the best ways to immerse yourself in the local culture is by engaging with the Toulousains themselves. Strike up a conversation with the locals as you visit the markets, cafes, or parks. The Toulousains are known for their friendly and welcoming nature, always eager to share their love for their city and its heritage.

Toulouse takes great pride in its artistic heritage. Art, music, and literature have played pivotal roles in shaping the city's identity. Attend local art exhibitions, concerts, and theater performances to witness firsthand the creative expression that permeates Toulouse's cultural scene. The city hosts numerous festivals and events throughout the year, offering opportunities to celebrate art in all its forms.

Exploring Toulouse's museums also provides insights into its cultural heritage. Museums like Musée des Augustins showcase an impressive collection of art spanning various periods, while Les Abattoirs exhibit contemporary and modern art. These cultural institutions offer a glimpse into the city's artistic evolution, connecting the past with the present.

A visit to Toulouse wouldn't be complete without experiencing its vibrant street life. Wander through the bustling streets of the city center, where you'll find local musicians, street performers, and artisans showcasing their talents. Joining the locals in the city's squares during festivals and markets is an excellent opportunity to witness the spirit of celebration that binds the community together.

Cuisine is an integral part of any culture, and Toulouse's gastronomy is a true reflection of its rich heritage. Sample traditional Toulousain dishes like Cassoulet, a hearty and savory stew, and indulge in the city's love for delicious pastries like "fenetra" and "croustade." Engaging with local chefs and learning the secrets of their culinary artistry is a delightful way to appreciate the depth of Toulouse's food culture.

Sports also play an essential role in the local culture, particularly rugby. Rugby holds a special place in the hearts of Toulousains, and attending a match at the Stade Toulousain, one of the most successful rugby clubs in Europe, is an exhilarating experience that connects you to the passion of the city's sporting community.

Respecting local customs and traditions is crucial when immersing yourself in any culture. In Toulouse, you'll notice a relaxed pace of life and an appreciation for taking time to savor moments. Embrace the art of "joie de vivre" and savoring life's simple pleasures as you connect with the Toulousain way of living.

getting to know the local culture in Toulouse is a journey of discovery and connection. Engaging with the city's history, art, cuisine, and people allows you to unravel the essence of the Pink City and experience the heartwarming embrace of its vibrant cultural tapestry. By embracing the local culture, you'll leave Toulouse not just as a visitor but as someone who has shared in the joy and spirit of this captivating city.

CHAPTER 1
EXPLORING TOULOUSE'S TOP ATTRACTIONS

Toulouse, with its rich history and captivating charm, boasts a plethora of top attractions that beckon travelers from all corners of the world. In this chapter, we will embark on a journey to explore some of the city's most iconic landmarks, immersing ourselves in the heritage and beauty that define the Pink City.

Marveling at Basilica of Saint-Sernin:
Our first stop takes us to the Basilica of Saint-Sernin, a masterpiece of Romanesque architecture and one of the largest remaining medieval churches in Europe. As we step into its hallowed halls, we are awestruck by the grandeur of its soaring vaults, ornate chapels, and magnificent rose windows. Delving into its history, we discover the relics of Saint Saturnin, the city's patron saint,

and learn about the significant role the basilica played in the pilgrimage routes of the Middle Ages.

Discovering the Beauty of Capitole de Toulouse:
Next on our itinerary is the iconic Capitole de Toulouse, an imposing building that serves as the city's town hall and a cultural hub. We marvel at the Neoclassical facade adorned with stunning sculptures and intricate details. Inside, we are greeted by the majestic Salle des Illustres, a gallery showcasing remarkable paintings celebrating Toulouse's illustrious history. Our exploration of this architectural gem takes us on a journey through time, highlighting the city's administrative and artistic significance.

Strolling Through Jardin des Plantes:
Amidst the urban landscape, the Jardin des Plantes offers a tranquil oasis where we can escape the city's hustle and bustle. As we meander through the meticulously landscaped gardens, fragrant flowers, and serene ponds, we immerse ourselves in the

beauty of nature. The Jardin des Plantes is not only a picturesque retreat but also a testament to Toulouse's appreciation for green spaces and the harmony between the city and nature.

Embracing Aerospace History at Cité de l'Espace:
Our journey takes a cosmic turn as we venture into the realm of space exploration at Cité de l'Espace. This futuristic museum and theme park offer a captivating journey through the history of aerospace, from the first steps on the Moon to cutting-edge space missions. Interactive exhibits and full-scale replicas of space vehicles ignite our curiosity, giving us a taste of what it's like to be an astronaut. Cité de l'Espace epitomizes Toulouse's reputation as "Aerospace Valley" and offers a unique perspective on humanity's quest for the stars.

Exploring Modern Art at Les Abattoirs:
Our artistic adventure continues at Les Abattoirs, a contemporary art museum housed in a former

slaughterhouse. Here, we encounter thought-provoking works of art from various avant-garde movements, representing the city's commitment to artistic innovation. As we admire abstract paintings, sculptures, and multimedia installations, we gain insight into Toulouse's contemporary art scene and its evolving cultural landscape.

Exploring Toulouse's top attractions allows us to unravel the city's history, art, and innovation. From ancient religious marvels to modern expressions of creativity, each attraction holds a unique story that contributes to the tapestry of the Pink City's allure. As we delve deeper into Toulouse's treasures, we find ourselves enchanted by the timeless beauty and enduring spirit of this captivating destination.

Marveling at Basilica of Saint-Sernin

As we approach the Basilica of Saint-Sernin, a sense of awe washes over us. This monumental Romanesque structure stands tall, a testament to the rich religious heritage of Toulouse. We are captivated by its imposing presence, with its red brick walls and elegant bell towers reaching towards the sky.

Stepping through its ancient doors, we are greeted by an atmosphere of serenity and spirituality. The interior of the basilica is nothing short of breathtaking, with soaring vaulted ceilings and intricately carved columns. The play of light and shadow creates a mesmerizing ambiance, instilling a sense of reverence as we explore its vastness.

Our eyes are drawn to the radiant stained glass windows that bathe the interior in a kaleidoscope of colors. Each window tells a story from biblical events to the lives of saints, revealing the centuries-old artistry that adorns this sacred space.

We make our way to the heart of the basilica, where the tomb of Saint Saturnin lies. This patron saint of Toulouse holds a significant place in the city's history and religious identity. Pilgrims from all over once flocked to Saint-Sernin to pay their respects and seek blessings. The tomb stands as a symbol of faith and devotion that has withstood the test of time.

Throughout the basilica, numerous chapels invite us to pause and reflect. Each chapel houses revered relics and exquisite artwork, revealing the deep spirituality that permeates every corner of Saint-Sernin.

Climbing up to the choir loft, we are rewarded with a breathtaking view of the nave below. The sheer grandeur of the basilica becomes even more apparent from this vantage point, allowing us to appreciate the architectural marvel that Saint-Sernin truly is.

As we exit the basilica, we take a moment to admire the cloister, a tranquil courtyard surrounded by ancient arches. The cloister serves as a peaceful retreat, inviting contemplation and tranquility amidst the bustling city.

Leaving the Basilica of Saint-Sernin, we carry with us a profound sense of connection to the past and a renewed appreciation for the enduring beauty of this historical treasure. The grandeur of its architecture and the spiritual aura within its walls leave an indelible mark on our hearts, forever associating the Pink City of Toulouse with the unforgettable marvel that is the Basilica of Saint-Sernin.

Discovering the Beauty of Capitole de Toulouse

The moment we set eyes on the grand facade of Capitole de Toulouse, we are drawn to its majestic splendor. Standing proudly in the heart of the city, this impressive building serves as both the town hall and a cultural center, embodying the essence of Toulouse's heritage and artistic soul.

As we approach, the Neoclassical architecture captivates us with its harmonious symmetry and intricate details. The elegant pink marble columns and statues adorned with allegorical figures evoke a sense of grace and refinement. The facade's grandeur is a testament to Toulouse's historical importance and its position as a city of great significance.

Stepping inside the Capitole, we are greeted by the breathtaking Salle des Illustres, a lavishly decorated hall adorned with magnificent paintings. The vivid murals depict the city's historical figures, events, and significant moments, offering a visual journey through Toulouse's illustrious past. This space not only serves as a celebration of the city's history but also as a tribute to the artists who have left their mark on Toulouse's cultural landscape.

The Capitole houses several important rooms, each exuding its unique charm. The Salle Henri Martin, dedicated to the renowned artist, showcases beautiful paintings depicting Toulouse's landscapes and historical scenes. The Salle Gervais, with its ornate wooden paneling and opulent chandeliers, offers an intimate setting for smaller gatherings and cultural events.

As we ascend the majestic staircase, we find ourselves in the Capitole's courtyard, a haven of tranquility amidst the bustling city. Here, a statue of the famous poet Pierre Goudouli presides over the space, reminding us of Toulouse's appreciation for literature and the arts.

Throughout the year, the Capitole serves as a vibrant venue for cultural events, concerts, and exhibitions. The enchanting setting becomes even more alive during festivals and celebrations, filling the air with music, dance, and laughter. We find ourselves immersed in the city's joie de vivre as we join the locals in these joyous gatherings.

The Capitole de Toulouse is not merely a building; it is the heart and soul of the city. It symbolizes Toulouse's resilience, artistic legacy, and commitment to celebrating its heritage. Whether one comes to admire its architectural splendor, witness the Salle des Illustres' masterpieces, or immerse themselves in the cultural events it hosts, the Capitole leaves an indelible impression on all who pass through its grand doors.

Leaving the Capitole, we carry with us a profound sense of appreciation for the beauty that this remarkable building represents. It is a tribute to the city's rich history and its people's enduring spirit, forever making the Capitole de Toulouse a cherished symbol of the Pink City's allure.

Strolling Through Jardin des Plantes

In the heart of Toulouse, an enchanting oasis awaits, a sanctuary of greenery and serenity known as the Jardin des Plantes. As I step into this botanical wonderland, the world outside fades away, and a sense of tranquility envelops me.

The pathways lead me on a meandering journey through a kaleidoscope of colors and shapes. Lush vegetation surrounds me, and the fragrance of blooming flowers dances on the breeze, transporting me to a realm of natural beauty. I find myself lost in the symphony of nature, where the gentle rustling of leaves and the chirping of birds become a soothing melody for my soul.

As I stroll further, I encounter hidden treasures scattered throughout the garden. A secluded bench beneath a canopy of trees beckons me to pause and ponder, while a quaint gazebo offers a picture-perfect view of the surrounding greenery.

Each corner seems to hold a secret waiting to be discovered, a surprise that adds to the garden's allure.

The centerpiece of the Jardin des Plantes is a serene pond, its still waters reflecting the majesty of the flora that surrounds it. Ducks glide gracefully across the surface, their presence adding a touch of whimsy to the peaceful scene. I sit by the pond's edge, mesmerized by the play of light on the water, and feel a sense of connectedness with nature that is both calming and uplifting.

Themed sections of the garden transport me to different corners of the world. Mediterranean flora takes me on a sensory journey to the shores of the Mediterranean Sea, while exotic blooms from distant lands ignite my curiosity and wonder. Each section presents a new story, a glimpse into the diverse beauty that nature offers.

As I continue my exploration, I encounter fellow wanderers, all drawn to this sanctuary of green.

Smiles exchanged and nods of appreciation shared create an unspoken bond, a collective understanding of the magic that the Jardin des Plantes bestows upon its visitors.

Beyond its captivating beauty, the garden serves as an educational space. Informative displays and interactive exhibits invite me to learn more about the wonders of the plant kingdom, deepening my appreciation for the delicate balance between humanity and nature.

As I bid farewell to the Jardin des Plantes, I carry with me a sense of renewal and harmony. This green haven has reminded me of the importance of preserving our connection with nature, offering a respite from the bustle of urban life. I leave with a promise to return, knowing that whenever I seek solace and a moment of peace, the Jardin des Plantes will welcome me back with open arms.

CHAPTER 2
TOULOUSE'S ART AND MUSEUMS

Toulouse's cultural tapestry is woven with threads of artistic brilliance and creative expression. In this chapter, we delve into the city's thriving art scene and explore its world-class museums that showcase a diverse range of masterpieces from various periods and genres.

Admiring Masterpieces at Musée des Augustins:
Our journey begins at the Musée des Augustins, housed within a former Augustinian monastery. This museum is a treasure trove of art, boasting an extensive collection of sculptures and paintings from the Middle Ages to the 20th century. We are mesmerized by the intricate details of medieval religious sculptures, and we find ourselves transported to different eras as we gaze at the paintings by renowned artists like Delacroix and Rembrandt. The museum's impressive setting and

carefully curated exhibits make it a true haven for art enthusiasts and history aficionados alike.

Immersing in Aerospace History at Cité de l'Espace: While exploring Toulouse's art, we encounter a unique blend of science and creativity at Cité de l'Espace. This innovative museum dedicated to space exploration and astronomy offers an interactive experience that sparks curiosity and wonder. We get a glimpse of the fascinating world beyond our planet through realistic exhibits, including full-scale replicas of space vehicles and space-themed attractions. Cité de l'Espace pays homage to Toulouse's reputation as "Aerospace Valley" and provides an opportunity to learn about humanity's exploration of the cosmos.

Exploring Modern Art at Les Abattoirs:
Our artistic journey continues at Les Abattoirs, a contemporary art museum housed in a former slaughterhouse. This cutting-edge institution showcases avant-garde works from the 20th and

21st centuries, presenting a thought-provoking perspective on modern art. As we walk through the museum's halls, we encounter abstract paintings, multimedia installations, and sculptures that challenge conventions and ignite our imaginations. Les Abattoirs is a vibrant testament to Toulouse's commitment to artistic innovation and its thriving contemporary art scene.

Toulouse's art and museums offer a profound glimpse into the city's creative spirit and its appreciation for artistic expression in all its forms. From medieval masterpieces to avant-garde creations, each museum reveals a facet of the Pink City's cultural identity, leaving us with a deeper appreciation for its rich heritage and artistic legacy. As we continue to explore the artistic wonders of Toulouse, we find ourselves immersed in a world of beauty, inspiration, and artistic brilliance that captivates the heart and enriches the soul.

Admiring Masterpieces at Musée des Augustins

The Musée des Augustins, housed within a former Augustinian monastery, is a captivating destination for art enthusiasts and history lovers alike. The museum boasts an impressive collection of masterpieces that span various periods and genres, offering a glimpse into the rich artistic heritage of Toulouse.

Visitors to the Musée des Augustins are immediately greeted by striking medieval religious sculptures. These exquisite works of art display exceptional craftsmanship, with intricate details that have stood the test of time. Each sculpture tells a unique story, depicting religious narratives that have inspired awe and reverence for generations.

Moving through the museum's galleries, visitors encounter a diverse array of paintings by celebrated artists. The collection includes works by Eugène

Delacroix, Rembrandt, and other notable figures, showcasing different artistic movements and styles. The vivid colors, expressive brushstrokes, and emotive compositions are a testament to the enduring power of visual storytelling.

One of the museum's highlights is its tribute to local artists from Toulouse. Paintings by Pierre Rivals, Henri Martin, and other regional talents are on display, offering insights into the city's unique artistic contribution and cultural identity.

The Musée des Augustins also celebrates the historical significance of its former monastery setting. The blend of sacred architecture with artistic treasures creates a contemplative ambiance, enhancing the appreciation of each masterpiece's beauty and historical context.

Throughout its corridors and alcoves, the museum surprises visitors with lesser-known gems waiting to be discovered. These hidden treasures provide an opportunity to delve deeper into art history and to appreciate the wealth of creativity that has shaped Toulouse's cultural landscape.

The Musée des Augustins stands as a testament to the enduring importance of art in human expression and understanding. It is a space where the past converges with the present, and where visitors can connect with the timeless beauty of masterpieces that continue to inspire and captivate. A visit to the Musée des Augustins is a journey through the heart and soul of art, leaving all who experience it with a profound appreciation for the depth and diversity of human creativity.

Immersing in Aerospace History at Cité de l'Espace

At Cité de l'Espace, the boundary between Earth and the cosmos fades away, and visitors are transported on an extraordinary journey through the history of space exploration and astronomy. This innovative museum in Toulouse offers an interactive and immersive experience that sparks curiosity and wonder, leaving a lasting impression on all who venture through its gates.

As visitors step into the vast premises of Cité de l'Espace, they are greeted by full-scale replicas of space vehicles that once roamed the far reaches of our solar system. The sight of rockets and space shuttles ignites a sense of awe, reminding us of humanity's relentless pursuit of the stars and our fascination with the unknown.

Inside the museum, interactive exhibits and multimedia displays provide an insight into the wonders of space and the achievements of space exploration. Visitors can virtually explore the surface of Mars, witness the formation of stars in distant galaxies, and even experience the feeling of weightlessness in a simulated spacewalk. These immersive experiences evoke a profound sense of wonder and instill a deeper appreciation for the vastness and complexity of the universe.

Cité de l'Espace pays homage to Toulouse's reputation as "Aerospace Valley," a hub for aerospace research and innovation. The museum serves as a tribute to the countless scientists, engineers, and astronauts who have contributed to humanity's quest to unlock the mysteries of space.

The museum's outdoor area features life-sized replicas of famous space stations, such as the Mir space station and the ISS (International Space Station). Visitors can explore the interior of these spacecraft and gain insight into the daily lives of astronauts as they conduct experiments and live in microgravity.

As visitors stroll through the Cité de l'Espace, they are inspired by the spirit of exploration and the dream of reaching for the stars. The museum offers a glimpse into the future of space travel, with exhibits on upcoming missions and cutting-edge technology that promises to shape the next era of space exploration.

Cité de l'Espace is more than a museum; it is a gateway to the universe, where the wonders of space and the history of human achievements in aerospace come alive. The experience leaves visitors with a sense of wonder and a renewed appreciation for the beauty and vastness of the cosmos. As we depart from Cité de l'Espace, we carry with us the knowledge that, in the quest for knowledge and discovery, the sky is no longer the limit, and the possibilities are truly infinite.

Exploring Modern Art at Les Abattoirs

Les Abattoirs, located in the heart of Toulouse, is an avant-garde museum that showcases an impressive collection of modern and contemporary art. Housed in a former slaughterhouse, the museum's innovative setting offers a unique backdrop for visitors to immerse themselves in the world of modern artistic expression.

As visitors step into Les Abattoirs, they are greeted by a vibrant and dynamic atmosphere. The museum's vast exhibition spaces host a diverse array of artworks that challenge conventions and push the boundaries of creativity. Abstract paintings, multimedia installations, sculptures, and video art are among the many artistic forms represented, showcasing the rich diversity of contemporary art.

The museum's collection includes works by both renowned artists and emerging talents. As visitors explore the galleries, they encounter thought-provoking pieces that invite introspection and interpretation. Each artwork conveys a distinct message or emotion, evoking a range of feelings from curiosity to contemplation.

One of the museum's highlights is its commitment to showcasing regional and local artists. Visitors have the opportunity to discover the vibrant art scene of Toulouse and the surrounding regions, fostering a sense of connection with the artistic community and the city's cultural identity.

Les Abattoirs is not only a place for contemplation and appreciation but also a hub for creativity and expression. The museum hosts regular exhibitions, workshops, and events that engage visitors in dialogue with contemporary art. The interactive nature of these programs encourages active participation and invites visitors to delve deeper into the world of modern art.

As visitors make their way through Les Abattoirs, they are inspired by the spirit of innovation and experimentation that permeates the space. The museum serves as a platform for artists to push the boundaries of their creativity, offering visitors a glimpse into the cutting-edge art of today.

Leaving Les Abattoirs, visitors carry with them a renewed appreciation for modern art and a sense of excitement about the ever-evolving world of contemporary creativity. The experience at the museum leaves a lasting impression, encouraging visitors to view art as a medium for exploring ideas, challenging perceptions, and celebrating the boundless potential of human imagination. As they depart from Les Abattoirs, visitors are inspired to continue their journey of exploration and discovery in the world of contemporary art and to celebrate the transformative power of artistic expression.

CHAPTER 3
CULINARY DELIGHTS OF TOULOUSE

Toulouse is not only a city of rich history and art but also a culinary paradise that tantalizes the taste buds of food enthusiasts from around the globe. In this chapter, we embark on a gastronomic adventure through the Pink City, savoring its delectable dishes and experiencing the essence of Toulousain cuisine.

Savoring the Iconic Cassoulet:
No culinary journey in Toulouse is complete without indulging in the iconic Cassoulet. This hearty dish is a symphony of flavors, featuring slow-cooked white beans, tender meat (typically duck, pork, and sausage), and aromatic herbs. The Cassoulet exemplifies the essence of Toulousain comfort food, and every bite takes us on a journey through the region's rustic culinary heritage.

Delighting in Toulouse's Beloved Pastries:

Toulouse takes immense pride in its delightful pastries, each a treasure trove of flavors and traditions. "Fenetra," a sweet pastry made with candied fruit and almonds, entices us with its irresistible sweetness. The "croustade," a flaky pastry filled with apples, transports us back in time with every bite. These delectable pastries offer a taste of Toulouse's culinary heritage, rooted in simplicity and reverence for the finest ingredients.

Reveling in Toulousain Charcuterie:
Toulouse's charcuterie is renowned for its authenticity and richness of flavors. From the savory "saucisse de Toulouse" to the delectable "jambon de Bayonne," the city's cured meats delight our palates with every savory morsel. The charcuterie showcases the region's dedication to preserving traditional techniques and the art of crafting mouthwatering delicacies.

Relishing Duck Confit and Foie Gras:

Toulouse's culinary prowess extends to its mastery of duck dishes. The succulent Duck Confit, slowly cooked in its own fat until tender, presents a delightful blend of textures and flavors. Equally celebrated is Toulouse's Foie Gras, a delicacy of rich, buttery goodness that showcases the city's expertise in the art of fine dining.

Indulging in Toulouse's Vibrant Market Scene:
One of the best ways to immerse oneself in the culinary delights of Toulouse is to explore its bustling markets. The Marché Victor Hugo and the Marché des Carmes offer an array of fresh produce, cheeses, and local specialties. Engaging with local vendors and sampling their offerings provides an authentic glimpse into Toulouse's food culture and the passion that drives its culinary artisans.

Pairing with Local Wines:
Toulouse's culinary delights are complemented by the region's exceptional wines. The nearby vineyards of Fronton and Gaillac produce a variety

of reds, whites, and rosés that perfectly complement the city's gastronomic offerings. A glass of locally produced wine is the ideal accompaniment to a sumptuous Toulousain meal, completing the culinary experience with finesse.

the culinary delights of Toulouse reflect a city that takes immense pride in its culinary heritage. From savory cassoulet to delicate pastries and flavorful charcuterie, Toulouse's cuisine is a celebration of its rich traditions and love for fine dining. As we explore the gastronomic treasures of the Pink City, we become enchanted by the warmth and flavors that define Toulousain cuisine, leaving us with an enduring appreciation for the art of savoring life's simple pleasures.

Sampling Traditional Toulousain Cuisine

Exploring the culinary wonders of Toulouse is an experience that indulges all the senses. The city's traditional cuisine offers a delightful blend of flavors, textures, and aromas that reflect the region's rich agricultural heritage and culinary traditions.

One cannot begin a culinary journey in Toulouse without savoring the iconic Cassoulet. This hearty dish, featuring slow-cooked white beans, tender meats, and fragrant herbs, embodies the essence of Toulousain comfort food. The flavors come together in a symphony of taste, leaving a lasting impression on the palate.

For those with a sweet tooth, Toulouse's beloved pastries are a must-try. The "Fenetra," a delightful pastry made with candied fruit and almonds, delights with its delightful sweetness. Meanwhile, the "croustade," filled with luscious apples, offers a delicate balance of textures and tastes that transport us to a bygone era.

The city's charcuterie is another culinary treasure waiting to be explored. From the savory "saucisse de Toulouse" to the flavorful "jambon de Bayonne," the cured meats are a testament to Toulouse's dedication to preserving traditional techniques. Each bite offers a taste of the region's authenticity and culinary heritage.

No exploration of Toulouse's cuisine is complete without savoring the delectable Duck Confit. Cooked to perfection in its own fat, the tender duck dish delights the palate with its richness and depth of flavor. Equally renowned is Toulouse's Foie Gras, a delicacy celebrated for its indulgent and buttery texture.

To truly immerse oneself in the local food culture, a visit to Toulouse's vibrant markets is a must. The Marché Victor Hugo and the Marché des Carmes showcase an array of fresh produce, cheeses, and local specialties. Engaging with passionate vendors and sampling their offerings provides an authentic glimpse into Toulouse's food scene.

As the culinary adventure unfolds, pairing the traditional dishes with locally produced wines is a delightful treat. The vineyards of Fronton and Gaillac offer a variety of reds, whites, and rosés that perfectly complement the flavors of Toulouse's cuisine, elevating the dining experience to new heights.

Sampling traditional Toulousain cuisine is an exploration of the city's soul and a celebration of its culinary artistry. Each dish and delicacy tells a story, offering a taste of history and the passion of its makers. The experience leaves a lasting impression on the palate and the heart, forever associating Toulouse with the joy of savoring life's simple and delicious pleasures.

Unveiling the Secrets of Cassoulet

Cassoulet, a dish that embodies the essence of Toulousain comfort food, is a culinary treasure with a rich history and a tapestry of flavors waiting to be discovered. As we delve into the secrets of Cassoulet, we are transported on a gastronomic journey that reveals the traditions and craftsmanship that make it an iconic dish of Toulouse.

At the heart of Cassoulet lies a harmonious blend of simple yet robust ingredients - tender white beans, succulent meats (typically duck, pork, and sausage), and a bouquet of aromatic herbs. The key to its exquisite taste lies in the slow and meticulous cooking process that allows the flavors to meld and develop into a symphony of taste.

Cassoulet is named after the vessel in which it is traditionally cooked - the cassole, a round earthenware dish. The slow cooking in this clay pot imparts a unique earthy flavor to the dish, enhancing its authenticity and rustic charm.

The origins of Cassoulet are rooted in the Languedoc region of France, where each town adds its unique touch to the recipe. Toulouse, as the culinary capital of the region, has perfected its version of Cassoulet, becoming synonymous with this cherished dish.

Unraveling the secrets of Cassoulet often leads to lively debates among locals and food enthusiasts alike. From the choice of meats to the cooking time and the right balance of seasonings, every detail contributes to the dish's character and complexity.

While the traditional preparation is a labor-intensive process that requires patience and attention to detail, the reward is a dish that speaks to the soul and offers a taste of Toulouse's culinary heritage.

As we savor Cassoulet in the cozy ambiance of a Toulousain bistro or family kitchen, we discover that this dish is more than just food; it is a celebration of tradition, family, and community. Sharing a pot of Cassoulet with loved ones is a cherished moment that brings people together and creates lasting memories.

Unveiling the secrets of Cassoulet reveals the soul of Toulouse, where culinary artistry and a deep-rooted love for good food converge. This iconic dish epitomizes the warm hospitality and passion for flavors that define the Pink City's gastronomic culture. As we take our last bite, we know that Cassoulet's secrets are best shared, creating a culinary legacy that transcends time and brings joy to all who indulge in its hearty embrace.

Enjoying the Vibrant Food Markets

In Toulouse, the vibrant food markets are a true feast for the senses, inviting locals and visitors alike to embark on a delightful culinary adventure. As we meander through the bustling stalls, the air is filled with the tantalizing aromas of fresh produce, artisanal cheeses, charcuterie, and pastries. The food markets of Toulouse are more than just places to shop; they are vibrant hubs that bring the city's culinary heritage to life.

One of the most renowned food markets is the Marché Victor Hugo, named after the famous French writer. This covered market, located in the heart of the city, is a treasure trove of gastronomic delights. The bustling atmosphere, colorful displays, and friendly vendors create an enchanting ambiance that beckons us to explore.

At the Marché Victor Hugo, we discover an abundance of fresh fruits and vegetables, sourced from local farmers who take immense pride in their produce. The vibrant colors and varieties of fruits and vegetables showcase the rich agricultural bounty of the region.

As we move further, we encounter stalls laden with an impressive selection of cheeses - soft, hard, and pungent - each with its unique story and flavor profile. The knowledgeable cheese vendors eagerly offer samples and provide insights into the art of cheese-making, allowing us to savor the diverse tastes of Toulousain fromage.

Charcuterie enthusiasts are in for a treat, as the market is adorned with an array of cured meats. The tantalizing aroma of saucisson and jambon de Bayonne fills the air, enticing us to taste these savory delights that reflect the region's passion for quality craftsmanship.

But it is not only savory treats that tempt our palates; Toulouse's food markets are also a haven for those with a sweet tooth. The sight of delicate pastries and mouthwatering desserts fills our hearts with joy. Fenetra, croustade, and other beloved treats are lovingly displayed, promising a delightful culinary indulgence.

The food markets are not just about buying ingredients; they are a place for community and connection. As we engage with the passionate vendors, we hear stories of family traditions, local recipes, and time-honored culinary techniques. The vendors' pride in their offerings is infectious, leaving us with a deeper appreciation for the city's food culture.

As we bid farewell to the vibrant food markets of Toulouse, we leave with bags full of fresh produce, cheeses, charcuterie, and pastries, but also with cherished memories and a taste of the city's culinary spirit. The experience of enjoying the vibrant food markets is a celebration of Toulouse's rich gastronomic heritage, where the love for good food and the joy of community converge in a delectable symphony that lingers in our hearts and on our palates for years to come.

CHAPTER 4
DAY TRIPS FROM TOULOUSE

In Toulouse, the vibrant food markets are a sensory delight, where the city's culinary culture comes alive. Exploring these bustling markets is a feast for the senses, offering a kaleidoscope of colors, aromas, and flavors that entice both locals and visitors alike.

The Marché Victor Hugo, located in the heart of the city, is a gastronomic haven where rows of stalls display an array of fresh produce, cheeses, meats, and artisanal products. The atmosphere is alive with the buzz of activity as vendors proudly present their offerings, each one eager to share the fruits of their labor and the stories behind their goods.

Wandering through the market's alleys, we are met with the sight of colorful fruits and vegetables, artfully arranged to entice our appetite. Local farmers proudly display their seasonal harvest, inviting us to taste the freshness of the region's bounty.

The aroma of freshly baked bread and pastries fills the air, leading us to artisan bakeries and pastry stalls. Here, we encounter Toulouse's beloved "Fenetra" and "croustade," each delicacy a testament to the city's rich pastry heritage.

Cheese lovers are in for a treat as they discover a treasure trove of regional cheeses. From creamy Roquefort to nutty Comté, the market showcases a diverse selection of French fromages that pair perfectly with local wines.

For those seeking charcuterie and meats, the Marché des Carmes is a must-visit destination. Here, skilled artisans offer an assortment of cured meats, sausages, and pâtés that showcase Toulouse's dedication to preserving culinary traditions.

The vibrant food markets not only offer an opportunity to savor local flavors but also to engage with the passionate vendors. As we interact with the merchants, they share their knowledge and pride in their products, adding a personal touch to our market experience.

The markets are more than just a place to buy food; they are a hub of community and conviviality. As we join locals in the search for the freshest ingredients, we become part of the rich tapestry of Toulouse's food culture.

Bringing our market finds back to our kitchen, we embark on culinary adventures, creating dishes that celebrate the bounty of the markets. The experience of savoring a meal made from local produce and artisanal products enhances our connection to the city and its culinary heritage.

Enjoying the vibrant food markets is an immersion into the heart of Toulouse's gastronomic soul. It is an invitation to celebrate the simple joys of good food, the camaraderie of sharing meals, and the appreciation for the artisans who enrich our lives with their culinary creations. As we bid farewell to the markets, we carry with us the memories of the vibrant colors, the tantalizing aromas, and the flavors that have left an indelible mark on our palates and hearts.

Discovering Carcassonne's Medieval Fortifications

Nestled in the beautiful region of Occitanie, Carcassonne is a picturesque city that transports visitors back in time with its medieval charm. The crowning jewel of Carcassonne is its magnificent medieval fortifications, which stand proudly as a testament to the city's rich history and strategic significance.

Carcassonne's imposing double-walled fortifications, punctuated by imposing towers and battlements, create an enchanting atmosphere, evoking tales of knights and princesses, and igniting the imagination. The Cité de Carcassonne, a UNESCO World Heritage site, beckons travelers to step into a world of medieval wonder.

The fortified city's labyrinth of cobbled streets and charming medieval buildings adds to the historic ambiance, creating a captivating environment for exploration. The walls, built between the 13th and 14th centuries, are a marvel of medieval engineering, designed to withstand sieges and protect the city's inhabitants. With 52 watchtowers and battlements, the defense system offers panoramic views of the surrounding countryside.

Carcassonne's fortifications served as a residence for the city's rulers, such as the Château Comtal, a medieval castle that still stands today. Inside its walls, visitors can find a treasure trove of artifacts and exhibits that reveal the story of Carcassonne's past.

As the sun sets over Carcassonne, the fortifications take on a magical glow, creating a fairy-tale ambiance that captivates all who walk its streets. Strolling along the ramparts at dusk, visitors are transported to a bygone era, where chivalry and valor were held in high esteem.

Today, Carcassonne's medieval fortifications continue to stand as an awe-inspiring testament to the resilience and ingenuity of its medieval inhabitants. The city's fortifications have weathered the test of time, preserving the legacy of the past for future generations to admire and appreciate.

Discovering Carcassonne's medieval fortifications is not just a journey through history but also an opportunity to be enchanted by the architectural wonders and immerse in a world of knights, kings, and tales of valor. As travelers bid adieu to this timeless city, they carry with them the memories of its storied past, forever etched in the enduring stones of its fortifications.

Exploring the Canal du Midi and its Surroundings

The Canal du Midi, a remarkable engineering marvel and a UNESCO World Heritage site, winds its way through the captivating landscapes of southern France, offering an enchanting journey for travelers seeking to immerse themselves in the region's beauty and history.

Stretching over 240 kilometers, the Canal du Midi was constructed in the 17th century under the visionary guidance of Pierre-Paul Riquet. Its purpose was to provide a safe and efficient trade route, connecting the Garonne River to the Mediterranean Sea. Today, it serves as a popular tourist destination, offering a peaceful and idyllic setting for exploration.

Cruising along the gentle waters of the canal, travelers are treated to a serene experience as they pass through scenic countryside, vineyards, and charming villages. The lush greenery along the banks adds to the tranquility, creating a soothing atmosphere that allows for a leisurely appreciation of the surrounding natural beauty.

For those seeking an active adventure, the towpaths alongside the canal provide perfect opportunities for cycling or walking. Exploring the paths on foot or by bike offers a chance to witness the scenic splendor up close and allows travelers to discover hidden gems that may be missed from the water.

As travelers journey along the canal, they encounter picturesque villages and towns, each with its unique character and history. These charming stops offer a glimpse into the local culture and provide opportunities to taste the region's delectable culinary delights and sample its renowned wines.

The Canal du Midi is also adorned with remarkable architectural structures, including historic stone bridges and elegant aqueducts that have stood the test of time. These engineering marvels are a testament to the ingenuity of their creators and add to the allure of the canal's journey.

Nature enthusiasts can revel in the abundant wildlife that thrives along the canal's banks. Birdwatchers can spot a variety of waterfowl, including herons and ducks, gracefully gliding on the water or nesting in the reeds.

The Canal du Midi offers a captivating and memorable exploration, allowing travelers to immerse themselves in the region's beauty and history. As they venture along the tranquil waters and picturesque landscapes, they gain a deeper appreciation for the timeless allure of this historical treasure and the natural wonders that surround it.

Escaping to the Scenic Pyrenees Mountains

The Pyrenees Mountains, situated between France and Spain, offer a breathtaking escape into a world of natural beauty and serene landscapes. This mountain range is a haven for nature enthusiasts, outdoor adventurers, and anyone seeking a tranquil retreat surrounded by untouched wilderness.

As we journey into the heart of the Pyrenees, we are greeted by majestic peaks, verdant valleys, and cascading waterfalls that paint a mesmerizing picture. The diverse terrain ensures that each step reveals a new and captivating panorama, encouraging us to explore deeper into its unspoiled terrain.

Hiking enthusiasts will find an abundance of trails to traverse, each leading to its unique treasures. Whether it's a leisurely stroll through alpine meadows or a challenging ascent to a towering summit, the Pyrenees cater to all levels of experience and fitness.

Wildlife enthusiasts will be delighted to encounter a variety of animals in their natural habitat, including Pyrenean chamois, ibex, marmots, and a rich diversity of bird species. The mountains provide a sanctuary for these creatures, allowing us to witness the wonders of the animal kingdom in a pristine environment.

In winter, the Pyrenees transform into a snow-covered wonderland, inviting skiers and snowboarders to enjoy the slopes. World-class ski resorts offer an array of winter sports activities, making the Pyrenees a sought-after destination for snow lovers.

Amidst its natural allure, the Pyrenees are adorned with charming mountain villages, each exuding a unique charm and cultural heritage. Traditional stone houses, cobblestone streets, and local markets offer a glimpse into the rich history and warm hospitality of the region's inhabitants.

The Pyrenees also hold a significant historical legacy, with ancient Romanesque churches and medieval fortresses dotting the landscape. These architectural wonders add to the cultural tapestry of the region, offering a blend of natural beauty and historical heritage.

Escaping to the scenic Pyrenees Mountains allows us to disconnect from the noise of modern life and reconnect with nature's tranquility. The mountains' splendor, combined with the opportunities for outdoor adventure and cultural exploration, create an experience that is both invigorating and serene. The Pyrenees stand as a testament to the enduring beauty of the natural world, reminding us of the importance of preserving these pristine environments for future generations to cherish and enjoy.

CHAPTER 5
TOULOUSE'S HIDDEN GEMS

Beyond the well-known landmarks and bustling streets lies a treasure trove of hidden gems waiting to be discovered in Toulouse. These lesser-known attractions offer a glimpse into the city's lesser-explored corners, providing a unique and enriching experience for intrepid travelers.

Musée Georges Labit: Nestled in a serene park, this hidden gem is a museum of Asian and Egyptian art. The collection includes ancient artifacts, sculptures, and art pieces, providing a fascinating insight into different cultures from across the globe.

Canal de Brienne: While the Canal du Midi takes center stage, the lesser-known Canal de Brienne offers a more intimate and tranquil ambiance. A stroll along its banks allows visitors to soak in the picturesque views and escape the city's hustle and bustle.

Hôtel d'Assézat: This elegant mansion houses the renowned Bemberg Foundation, showcasing an impressive art collection. The beautifully restored building itself is a sight to behold, offering a glimpse into Toulouse's architectural heritage.

Jardin Japonais: Tucked away behind the Compans Caffarelli park, this serene Japanese garden is a peaceful oasis in the heart of the city. Its meticulously landscaped gardens, tranquil pond, and traditional Japanese elements create a zen-like atmosphere.

Hôtel-Dieu Saint-Jacques: A hidden gem of Toulouse's historical architecture, this former hospital is a prime example of 16th-century Renaissance style. Its stunning courtyard and intricate façade make it a must-visit for architecture enthusiasts.

Les Abattoirs - Musée d'Art Moderne et Contemporain: While the city's art scene often centers around traditional museums, Les Abattoirs stands out as a contemporary art haven. This converted slaughterhouse houses an impressive collection of modern and contemporary artworks.

Carmes Market: Unlike the more famous Victor Hugo Market, the Carmes Market is a local favorite, offering a more authentic and intimate experience. Here, visitors can savor the sights, scents, and flavors of regional produce and artisanal products.

Pont Neuf: Although its name means "New Bridge," Pont Neuf is actually Toulouse's oldest bridge, dating back to the 16th century. Its historical significance and unique design make it an intriguing spot for history enthusiasts and photographers.

Les Jacobins: Often overshadowed by the Basilica of Saint-Sernin, this medieval monastery is a hidden gem of Gothic architecture. Its elegant cloister and stunning palm-tree-like pillars in the church make it a hidden treasure worth exploring.

Cité de l'Espace Nocturnal Visits: While Cité de l'Espace is a well-known attraction, its nocturnal visits offer a completely different experience. Exploring the wonders of space under the starry night sky adds an extra touch of magic to the visit.

Toulouse's hidden gems are a testament to the city's multifaceted character and offer a chance to delve deeper into its rich history, art, and culture. Exploring these off-the-beaten-path treasures ensures that travelers have a truly authentic and unforgettable experience in the Pink City.

Off-the-Beaten-Path Neighborhoods

While the main attractions in Toulouse are undeniably captivating, exploring the city's off-the-beaten-path neighborhoods unveils a side of Toulouse that few visitors get to experience. These lesser-known areas are teeming with local charm, unique character, and hidden delights waiting to be discovered.

Saint-Cyprien: Situated on the left bank of the Garonne River, Saint-Cyprien is a vibrant neighborhood known for its lively atmosphere and eclectic mix of cultures. Here, visitors can meander through colorful streets adorned with street art and stumble upon quaint cafes and boutiques.

Saint-Aubin: Nestled between the Capitole Square and the Canal du Midi, Saint-Aubin exudes a bohemian vibe. This artsy district is home to an array of independent galleries, artisanal workshops, and vintage stores, making it a haven for art enthusiasts and collectors.

Quartier des Chalets: A true hidden gem, Quartier des Chalets is a residential neighborhood with a quaint village feel. Its charming architecture, tree-lined streets, and peaceful squares make it a perfect escape from the city's hustle.

La Terrasse: Perched on a hill overlooking the Garonne River, La Terrasse offers breathtaking panoramic views of Toulouse. This elevated neighborhood is a serene escape, perfect for a leisurely walk or a quiet moment of contemplation.

Les Minimes: Located north of the city center, Les Minimes is a laid-back district with a youthful vibe. This area is home to the Université Toulouse II - Le Mirail, giving it a lively and dynamic atmosphere with a mix of students and locals.

Croix-Daurade: A residential area with a touch of rural charm, Croix-Daurade feels like a quaint village within the city. Strolling through its streets, visitors may encounter hidden parks and gardens that offer peaceful retreats from urban life.

Amidonniers: Bordering the Garonne River, Amidonniers is a lesser-known neighborhood that boasts a mix of traditional and modern architecture. Its proximity to the riverfront makes it an ideal spot for a relaxing riverside stroll.

Les Carmes: Nestled between the Capitole Square and the Garonne River, Les Carmes is a charming district with narrow streets and historic buildings. It offers a more relaxed ambiance compared to the bustling city center.

Bonnefoy: This multicultural neighborhood is a melting pot of cultures and flavors. Its diverse community is reflected in the array of ethnic restaurants and shops that line its streets.

Lardenne: A residential area in the western part of Toulouse, Lardenne is known for its tranquility and suburban charm. It offers a delightful contrast to the city center, making it an ideal spot for a peaceful escape.

Exploring Toulouse's off-the-beaten-path neighborhoods not only reveals the city's diverse character but also provides a more intimate and authentic experience. These hidden corners offer a chance to connect with the local culture, discover charming streets, and create unforgettable memories off the tourist trail.

Unique Boutiques and Craft Shops

Toulouse is a city brimming with creativity, and nowhere is this more evident than in its unique boutiques and craft shops. These hidden gems offer a delightful shopping experience, where visitors can find one-of-a-kind treasures, locally crafted goods, and artisanal creations that showcase the city's vibrant artistic spirit.

Boutiques in Saint-Cyprien: The Saint-Cyprien neighborhood is a hub of artistic expression, and its boutiques reflect this creative energy. Here, visitors can discover handcrafted jewelry, eclectic fashion, and artistic home decor, all carefully curated by local designers and makers.

Artisanal Chocolate Shops: Toulouse is renowned for its chocolatiers who infuse passion and craftsmanship into every delectable treat. Artisanal chocolate shops, like Maison Pillon and Chocolaterie Didier, offer a wide array of exquisite chocolates and pralines that tantalize the taste buds.

Art Galleries in Saint-Aubin: Saint-Aubin is a paradise for art enthusiasts, with numerous art galleries showcasing works by local and international artists. These galleries are a treasure trove of paintings, sculptures, and mixed media creations that captivate the imagination.

Bookshops with a Vintage Flair: For book lovers, Toulouse boasts charming bookshops with a vintage flair, such as Ombres Blanches and Les Abattoirs. These literary havens invite visitors to browse through shelves filled with old and new volumes, making them perfect spots for literary discoveries.

Pottery and Ceramics Studios: Craft shops like Terre de Pastel and Atelier Terre Mêlée celebrate the art of pottery and ceramics. Visitors can find beautifully handcrafted tableware, vases, and decorative pieces that highlight the skill and creativity of local artisans.

Artistic Stationery Stores: If you're in search of unique stationery and paper goods, Toulouse's boutique stationery stores like Le Petit Souk and Papeterie Fontaine offer a delightful selection of artistic notebooks, pens, and greeting cards.

Vintage and Retro Shops: Vintage and retro enthusiasts will be delighted by Toulouse's array of thrift stores and vintage boutiques. Places like Emmaüs Boutique Vintage and Friperie La Fée Verte offer a treasure trove of clothing, accessories, and decor items from yesteryears.

Perfumeries with a Local Touch: Toulouse has a rich heritage of perfumery, and shops like Le Couvent des Minimes and Maison de la Violette capture the essence of local scents. Visitors can indulge in unique fragrances and cosmetics inspired by the region's natural elements.

Craft Beer Shops: Craft beer aficionados can explore the city's independent beer shops, such as Biérocratie and Saveur-Bière, where they can find a wide selection of locally brewed beers and ales with distinctive flavors.

Quirky Gift Shops: Toulouse's quirky gift shops, like La Cité des Objets Perdus and Les 2 Soeurs, offer an eclectic mix of fun and original souvenirs, ranging from quirky trinkets to stylish homewares.

Exploring Toulouse's unique boutiques and craft shops is an enchanting journey into the city's artistic soul. Each shop tells a story of passion, creativity, and the dedication of local artisans, making every find a cherished memento of the Pink City's vibrant and imaginative spirit.

Lesser-Known Landmarks with Fascinating Stories

Toulouse is a city with a rich history and a plethora of landmarks that tell fascinating stories. While some landmarks may be lesser-known compared to the iconic sites, they are no less captivating in their historical significance and cultural tales.

Le Bazacle: Situated on the Garonne River, Le Bazacle was once a bustling trading post and a symbol of Toulouse's economic prosperity in the Middle Ages. Today, the site houses a hydroelectric power plant and a museum that narrates the river's importance in shaping the city's destiny.

Hôtel du Vieux Raisin: This 16th-century mansion boasts an intriguing history and is believed to have connections to the infamous Knights Templar. Its intricate architecture and unique wooden galleries offer a glimpse into Toulouse's medieval past.

Musée du Vieux Toulouse: Housed in a historic Renaissance building, this museum showcases Toulouse's local history through an array of artifacts, documents, and objects. It provides a captivating journey into the city's heritage and cultural evolution.

La Grave: This riverside building once served as a hospital and later as a refuge for the poor. Today, La Grave is a cultural center, and its beautiful courtyard hosts open-air concerts and events that bring life to this historic landmark.

Port Saint-Sauveur: An impressive feat of engineering, Port Saint-Sauveur was constructed during the 17th century to connect the Canal du Midi to the Garonne River. Its construction was an essential step in developing Toulouse's role as a significant trading hub.

Musée Saint-Raymond: Though not as well-known as other museums, Musée Saint-Raymond offers a remarkable collection of Roman and medieval artifacts. Its exhibits shed light on the city's Roman origins and its subsequent evolution during the Middle Ages.

Le Pont Saint-Michel: This picturesque bridge not only provides beautiful views of the Garonne River but also has an intriguing past. It was once the site of a medieval wooden bridge that was destroyed and rebuilt several times due to floods and conflicts.

Place Saint-Pierre: This lively square is a popular spot for nightlife and social gatherings, but it also holds historical significance. It was the site of religious processions during the Middle Ages, and today, it continues to be a hub of social activity and cultural events.

Chapelle des Carmélites: Hidden within the Carmes neighborhood, this charming chapel is a hidden gem with a tranquil ambiance. Its historical importance and beautiful interior make it a serene retreat within the heart of the city.

Porte du Grand Rond: One of Toulouse's remaining city gates, the Porte du Grand Rond was part of the city's fortifications in the 17th century. Today, it stands as a reminder of the city's medieval past and adds character to the surrounding neighborhood.

Exploring Toulouse's lesser-known landmarks unveils a tapestry of historical tales and cultural heritage that adds depth to the city's allure. These hidden gems invite visitors to delve deeper into the layers of Toulouse's past and appreciate the significance of its diverse historical landmarks.

CHAPTER 6
OUTDOOR ADVENTURES IN TOULOUSE

Toulouse is not only a city of history and culture but also a paradise for outdoor enthusiasts. From scenic hikes to adrenaline-pumping activities, the Pink City offers a wide array of outdoor adventures that allow visitors to explore the region's natural beauty and revel in thrilling experiences.

Canal du Midi Cycling: Rent a bike and embark on a leisurely cycling expedition along the picturesque Canal du Midi. The tree-lined towpaths and charming locks make for a scenic and relaxing ride, perfect for cyclists of all ages and abilities.

Kayaking on the Garonne River: Get a unique perspective of Toulouse by kayaking on the Garonne River. Paddle under historic bridges, admire the city's architecture from the water, and experience the serene beauty of the river.

Hiking in the Pyrenees: The Pyrenees Mountains, within easy reach of Toulouse, offer an abundance of hiking trails. Whether you're a seasoned hiker or a casual nature lover, the Pyrenees have something to offer for everyone, from easy walks to challenging mountain treks.

Paragliding over the Countryside: Experience the thrill of paragliding and enjoy breathtaking views of the Toulouse countryside from above. Tandem paragliding experiences are available for those who want to soar through the skies with an experienced instructor.

Adventure Parks: Toulouse and its surrounding areas boast adventure parks like Cazères Aventure and Vertilac, where visitors can engage in activities such as ziplining, rope courses, and tree-climbing challenges.

Rock Climbing in Auzat: Located near Toulouse, Auzat offers excellent rock climbing opportunities for both beginners and experienced climbers. The stunning natural setting and challenging routes make it a popular spot for climbers.

Hot Air Balloon Rides: Take to the skies in a hot air balloon and experience the region's beauty from a different perspective. A hot air balloon ride offers a peaceful and breathtaking journey over the picturesque landscapes of Toulouse.

Horseback Riding in the Countryside: Discover the scenic countryside around Toulouse on horseback. Many equestrian centers offer guided rides through vineyards, forests, and meadows, allowing you to connect with nature in a unique way.

Picnicking by the Garonne: Enjoy a relaxing afternoon with a picnic by the Garonne River. There are several parks and green spaces along the riverbanks, providing the perfect setting for a leisurely outdoor meal with friends or family.

Stand-Up Paddleboarding: Try stand-up paddleboarding on the Canal du Midi or the Garonne River. It's a fun and accessible way to enjoy the water and get a full-body workout while taking in the city's beautiful surroundings.

Toulouse's outdoor adventures cater to all levels of fitness and interests, offering an exhilarating escape into nature and a chance to create unforgettable memories amidst the city's stunning landscapes. Whether you seek adrenaline-pumping activities or serene nature experiences, Toulouse has something to satisfy every outdoor adventurer.

Cycling Along the Canal du Midi

Embarking on a cycling journey along the Canal du Midi is a delightful way to immerse oneself in the beauty and history of the region. Stretching over 240 kilometers from Toulouse to the Mediterranean Sea, the Canal du Midi is a UNESCO World Heritage site and a testament to human ingenuity and engineering.

The tree-lined towpaths flanking the canal provide a picturesque and leisurely route for cyclists of all levels. Renting a bike in Toulouse or bringing your own, you set off on a two-wheeled adventure that takes you through charming villages, vineyards, and tranquil countryside.

As you pedal along, the gentle waters of the canal accompany you, reflecting the changing skies and offering a sense of serenity. The smooth path makes for a comfortable ride, allowing you to focus on the stunning landscapes and historical landmarks that line the route.

Passing through ancient locks and picturesque bridges, you connect with the canal's rich history. Built in the 17th century, the Canal du Midi was a visionary project by Pierre-Paul Riquet, linking the Atlantic Ocean to the Mediterranean Sea. Today, it stands as a masterpiece of engineering and an emblem of the region's cultural heritage.

Cycling along the canal, you encounter welcoming villages that offer delightful rest stops. Local cafes and restaurants beckon with their regional specialties, inviting you to savor the flavors of Occitan cuisine. A leisurely lunch by the water, enjoying the peaceful ambiance, becomes a cherished part of your journey.

For history enthusiasts, the Canal du Midi boasts ancient Romanesque churches, historic mansions, and charming lockkeeper's houses that dot the route. Each landmark tells a story of the canal's past and adds to the enchantment of your ride.

The Canal du Midi also offers opportunities to share your adventure with fellow travelers and locals. Along the way, you may encounter other cyclists, boaters, and friendly residents who share a passion for this unique and enchanting route.

As you continue your cycling odyssey, the landscape gradually changes, offering diverse scenery from vineyards and sunflower fields to cypress-lined paths and gently rolling hills. Each kilometer presents a new vista to explore and appreciate.

Cycling along the Canal du Midi is more than just a bike ride; it's a journey through time, nature, and culture. Whether you opt for a short day trip or an extended expedition, this cycling adventure leaves you with a profound appreciation for the beauty of the region and the legacy of its engineering marvel.

Boating on the Garonne River

Boating on the Garonne River is a serene and enchanting experience that allows visitors to appreciate the natural beauty and historical charm of Toulouse from a unique perspective. The Garonne River, which flows through the heart of the city, has been a vital lifeline for Toulouse throughout its history.

Embarking on a boat trip, whether on a traditional barge or a modern river cruise, provides a tranquil escape from the bustling city streets. As you glide along the gentle waters, you can feel the rhythm of the river and witness the city's landmarks unfold before your eyes.

The scenic riverbanks are adorned with a tapestry of architectural wonders, ranging from centuries-old bridges like Pont Neuf to modern buildings that harmoniously blend with the historical landscape. Each passing moment offers a new vista, capturing the essence of Toulouse's rich heritage and contemporary vibrancy.

As you drift along the Garonne, you gain insight into the city's historical significance and its role as a major commercial and cultural hub. The river was crucial for trade and transportation, and it played a significant role in shaping Toulouse's identity.

The boat journey offers ample opportunities to capture stunning photographs of the city's iconic landmarks reflected in the tranquil waters. The sight of the city's silhouette, with its elegant spires and rooftops, creates an enduring memory of your boating adventure.

Throughout the voyage, you are accompanied by the soothing sounds of the river and the gentle lapping of the water against the boat's hull. This immersive experience invites moments of reflection and appreciation for the beauty of nature and the city's architectural heritage.

Boating on the Garonne also provides an excellent opportunity for socializing and connecting with fellow travelers. Whether you're on a shared cruise or renting a boat with friends and family, the camaraderie and shared experience enhance the joy of the journey.

As the boat glides along, the city's vibrant riverfront comes to life, with locals and visitors enjoying leisurely walks, picnics, and various water-based activities. The river's banks are dotted with parks, gardens, and terraces, inviting you to disembark and explore the riverside charms.

A boating adventure on the Garonne River leaves you with a deep appreciation for Toulouse's intricate connection to its waterways. It's a journey that immerses you in the city's past and present, revealing the allure of Toulouse's river heritage and the timeless beauty of its urban landscape.

Hiking in the Quaint Countryside

Just a short distance away from the vibrant city of Toulouse lies a tranquil countryside, beckoning hikers to explore its natural beauty and idyllic landscapes. Hiking in the quaint countryside surrounding Toulouse offers a welcome escape from the urban hustle, immersing you in the serenity of nature and revealing hidden gems waiting to be discovered.

The countryside trails are a hiker's paradise, catering to all levels of experience and fitness. Whether you're an avid trekker seeking challenging ascents or a leisurely stroller in search of gentle paths, the countryside has something to offer for everyone.

As you set foot on the trails, you are enveloped by the soothing sounds of chirping birds, rustling leaves, and the gentle flow of streams. The air is infused with the fragrance of wildflowers and the scent of fresh earth, creating a sensory symphony that awakens the senses.

The quaint countryside boasts a diverse array of landscapes, from rolling hills and meadows to dense woodlands and vineyards. Each step brings new vistas to admire, and at every turn, you encounter picturesque scenes that beg to be captured on camera.

The countryside is rich in history and cultural heritage, with charming villages and ancient ruins tucked away along the trails. Stumbling upon old stone churches, historic châteaux, and traditional farmhouses adds an extra layer of fascination to your hiking adventure.

As you ascend to higher vantage points, you are rewarded with panoramic views of the countryside stretching out before you. The sight of lush valleys, meandering rivers, and distant hills rolling into the horizon instills a sense of wonder and gratitude for the beauty of nature.

Hiking in the quaint countryside is also an opportunity to encounter local wildlife. Spotting deer, rabbits, and various bird species in their natural habitat adds to the sense of connection with the outdoors.

For those seeking a taste of local flavors, the countryside is a treasure trove of gastronomic delights. Many hiking trails pass by vineyards and orchards, offering a chance to sample regional wines, fruits, and other locally-produced delicacies.

Hiking in the countryside is not just about the destination but the journey itself. The peaceful ambiance, the company of fellow hikers, and the feeling of being in harmony with nature create a profound and rejuvenating experience.

Whether you embark on a short afternoon hike or a multi-day trek, hiking in the quaint countryside around Toulouse provides an opportunity to escape, recharge, and connect with the beauty of the natural world. It's an invitation to slow down, breathe in the fresh air, and relish the simple joys of exploration amidst the serene and enchanting countryside.

CHAPTER 7
TOULOUSE'S FESTIVALS AND EVENTS

Toulouse is a city that knows how to celebrate, and its calendar is filled with vibrant festivals and events that reflect the city's lively spirit and rich cultural heritage. Throughout the year, locals and visitors alike come together to partake in these festivities, creating an atmosphere of joy, camaraderie, and a shared appreciation for art, music, and tradition.

Festival Occitània: Celebrating the Occitan culture, Festival Occitània is a vibrant event that takes place in late August. This festival showcases the region's heritage through music, dance, theater, and crafts. Visitors can immerse themselves in the distinct traditions of Occitania, experiencing the unique charm of this ancient culture.

Toulouse Carnival: In February or March, Toulouse comes alive with the Toulouse Carnival. Colorful parades, masked balls, and lively street performances fill the city with merriment. This beloved event captures the essence of carnival traditions, offering a wonderful opportunity for both children and adults to revel in the festive spirit.

Rio Loco Festival: Celebrating world music and cultures, the Rio Loco Festival takes place in June along the Garonne River. Musicians from across the globe gather to perform in this dynamic event, showcasing the diverse sounds and rhythms of different cultures.

Toulouse Plages: During the summer months, Toulouse Plages transforms the city into a beachside oasis. Along the banks of the Garonne River, sandy beaches, deck chairs, and refreshing water activities create a beach vacation atmosphere in the heart of the city.

Toulouse International Organ Festival: Music enthusiasts are treated to the Toulouse International Organ Festival, which takes place in September and October. This prestigious event attracts world-class organists who perform in Toulouse's historic churches, showcasing the city's rich musical heritage.

Festival Cinespaña: Devoted to Spanish and Latin American cinema, Festival Cinespaña is an annual celebration held in October. Film screenings, director Q&A sessions, and cultural events contribute to the festival's success, drawing cinephiles from far and wide.

Toulouse Game Show: For fans of pop culture, comics, video games, and sci-fi, the Toulouse Game Show is a much-anticipated event. Held in November, this extravaganza features cosplay competitions, meet-and-greets with celebrities, and a wide range of interactive activities.

Marathon des Mots: Celebrating literature, the Marathon des Mots is a literary festival held in June. Writers, poets, and intellectuals converge in Toulouse to share their works, participate in readings, and engage in thought-provoking discussions.

Christmas Markets: In December, Toulouse embraces the festive season with charming Christmas markets that pop up throughout the city. Visitors can browse through stalls selling holiday decorations, artisanal crafts, and delectable treats, creating a magical ambiance that warms the heart.

Floralies Internationales: Held every four years, the Floralies Internationales showcases the city's passion for floral artistry. Spectacular displays of flowers and plants transform Toulouse into a botanical wonderland, enchanting visitors with its beauty and creativity.

Toulouse's festivals and events offer a kaleidoscope of experiences that celebrate the city's culture, arts, and joie de vivre. From traditional rituals to modern celebrations, each event contributes to the tapestry of Toulouse's dynamic and vibrant character, inviting everyone to join in the festivities and make cherished memories in the Pink City.

Celebrating the Violet Festival

In late February, Toulouse comes alive with the enchanting fragrance and vibrant colors of violets during the annual Violet Festival. This unique celebration pays homage to the delicate flower that holds a special place in the heart of the city and its inhabitants.

The Violet Festival dates back to the 19th century when violets were an essential part of Toulouse's economy, particularly in the perfume industry. The city's mild climate provided the perfect conditions for violet cultivation, and fields of violet blossoms adorned the surrounding countryside.

Today, the Violet Festival continues to celebrate this floral heritage with a series of festivities that captivate locals and visitors alike. The festival takes place over a weekend, offering a plethora of events, activities, and delicious treats centered around violets.

The heart of the Violet Festival is the Marché aux Violettes (Violet Market), where vendors display an array of violet-themed products. From fresh violet bouquets and violet-infused perfumes to violet-flavored chocolates and violet liqueurs, the market is a sensory delight for flower enthusiasts and food lovers alike.

One of the highlights of the festival is the election of La Reine des Violettes (The Violet Queen). This beauty pageant crowns a young woman who embodies the spirit of the festival and serves as an ambassador for Toulouse's violets throughout the year.

During the Violet Festival, the city's historic streets and squares are adorned with violet-themed decorations and floral displays. Parades featuring flower-covered floats wind through the city, creating a festive and colorful spectacle.

Visitors can also explore workshops and demonstrations where they can learn about traditional violet cultivation and perfume-making techniques. This hands-on experience provides a deeper appreciation for the flower's cultural significance in the region.

The culinary delights of the Violet Festival are a highlight for food enthusiasts. Local chefs and bakers create an array of violet-inspired treats, such as violet macarons, candied violets, violet-flavored ice cream, and more. These delicacies not only tantalize the taste buds but also celebrate the flower's unique and delicate flavor.

The Violet Festival is not just a celebration of a flower; it is a celebration of Toulouse's rich heritage, culture, and sense of community. The festival brings people together, fostering a sense of pride and unity in the city's traditions and identity.

For locals, the Violet Festival is a cherished tradition, and for visitors, it is an opportunity to immerse themselves in the authentic and charming ambiance of Toulouse. Whether you have a passion for flowers, history, or simply wish to experience the joy of a unique cultural celebration, the Violet Festival is an enchanting and unforgettable experience in the Pink City.

Joining the Carnival of Toulouse

As winter bids farewell and the spirit of celebration fills the air, Toulouse bursts into a riot of colors, music, and laughter with the Carnival of Toulouse. This exuberant festival, celebrated annually in February or March, ignites the city with a contagious energy, inviting locals and visitors alike to partake in a joyous and unforgettable experience.

The Carnival of Toulouse is a time-honored tradition that dates back centuries, and its roots can be traced to ancient pagan celebrations that marked the end of winter and the beginning of spring. Today, the carnival has evolved into a spectacular event that showcases the city's creativity, diversity, and joie de vivre.

The highlight of the carnival is the Grande Parade, a vibrant procession of floats, costumed performers, and marching bands that wind their way through the streets of Toulouse. The floats, adorned with elaborate decorations and larger-than-life characters, serve as colorful canvases that depict various themes, from folklore and history to fantasy and whimsy.

The spirit of the carnival infects everyone, and participants of all ages don their most imaginative and eccentric costumes. From fairytale characters and mythical creatures to superheroes and historical figures, the streets become a living tapestry of creativity and self-expression.

Children, too, play a central role in the carnival, with schools and community groups joining in the festivities. Little ones don their favorite costumes, and families come together to share in the joy of the occasion.

As the parade makes its way through the city, the crowds join in the revelry, dancing to lively music and cheering on the performers. Laughter and excitement fill the air, and a sense of unity and camaraderie binds everyone present.

Street vendors offer a variety of treats and carnival delights, from cotton candy and candied apples to savory snacks and refreshing drinks. The tantalizing scents wafting through the air add to the festive ambiance and heighten the senses.

Throughout the carnival, impromptu street performances, acrobatic displays, and artistic showcases surprise and delight onlookers. The creative and spontaneous spirit of the festival creates an atmosphere of wonder and magic around every corner.

The Carnival of Toulouse culminates with the ritual burning of the "Caramentran," a symbolic figure representing the end of winter. This ritual, known as "Le Jugement de Caramentran," symbolizes the rebirth of spring and the triumph of light over darkness.

Joining the Carnival of Toulouse is not just a celebration; it is an immersive experience that connects you with the heart and soul of the city. Whether you're a participant in the parade, an enthusiastic spectator, or simply an eager reveler, the carnival leaves an indelible mark, infusing you with the vibrant spirit of Toulouse and creating cherished memories to last a lifetime.

Experiencing the Spectacle of Fête de la Musique

On the longest day of the year, June 21st, the city of Toulouse transforms into a vibrant and harmonious stage as it celebrates Fête de la Musique, a nationwide music festival that originated in France. This joyous event invites music lovers of all ages and backgrounds to revel in the magic of music, turning every corner of the city into a live concert venue.

Fête de la Musique is a celebration of the universal language of music, embracing all genres and styles. From classical to jazz, rock to hip-hop, folk to electronic, and everything in between, the festival showcases the diversity and richness of the musical landscape.

As the sun sets and the city's streets come alive, musicians and bands of all kinds set up impromptu stages in public squares, parks, street corners, and even in front of iconic landmarks. The air is charged with anticipation and excitement as the first notes of music fill the atmosphere.

Visitors to Toulouse are in for a treat as they embark on a musical journey through the city. The main square, Place du Capitole, is a focal point of the festivities, with performances that range from classical symphonies to lively dance beats. The majestic backdrop of the Capitole building adds an air of grandeur to the musical spectacle.

As you wander through the city, you'll stumble upon hidden gems: a jazz quartet performing in a quaint courtyard, a rock band belting out anthems in a bohemian bar, or a group of street performers captivating passersby with their unique sounds.

The festival brings together professional musicians, amateur performers, and even music enthusiasts who simply bring their instruments to join in the spontaneous jam sessions. The spirit of camaraderie and shared passion for music create a sense of unity that transcends language and cultural barriers.

Throughout the night, the streets of Toulouse come alive with the sounds of laughter, applause, and the hum of conversation as people gather to enjoy the music, dance, and celebrate the joy of life.

One of the unique aspects of Fête de la Musique is the participatory nature of the event. It encourages anyone and everyone to pick up an instrument, sing a song, or share their musical talent with the world. As a result, the festival is a celebration of creativity and inclusivity, where everyone is invited to become a part of the musical tapestry.

The Fête de la Musique in Toulouse is not just a festival; it is an experience that resonates with the heart and soul of the city. It encapsulates the spirit of unity, joy, and artistic expression, making it an unforgettable celebration of music that leaves a lasting impression on all who partake in its magic.

CONCLUSION

As we come to the end of our journey through Toulouse, it is evident that the Pink City is a captivating destination that weaves together history, culture, and a zest for life. From its rich architectural heritage to its vibrant festivals and events, Toulouse offers a delightful array of experiences that cater to every traveler's desires.

In "Toulouse Travel Guide," we explored the city's iconic landmarks, such as the Basilica of Saint-Sernin and Capitole de Toulouse, marveling at their historical significance and architectural splendor. We strolled through the serene Jardin des Plantes and immersed ourselves in the city's artistic treasures at Musée des Augustins and Les Abattoirs.

The Pink City's culinary delights proved to be a highlight, as we savored traditional Toulousain cuisine and unveiled the secrets of the famous

Cassoulet. Exploring the bustling food markets allowed us to experience the region's gastronomic diversity and indulge in its vibrant flavors.

Venturing beyond the city, we discovered Carcassonne's medieval fortifications and admired the scenic beauty of the Pyrenees Mountains. The serene surroundings of the Canal du Midi and the scenic countryside beckoned us to embrace the outdoors through cycling, boating, and hiking adventures.

The city's hidden gems charmed us with off-the-beaten-path neighborhoods and unique boutiques, revealing Toulouse's creative spirit and artistic soul. We joined the lively celebrations of the Violet Festival and experienced the joy of music during the Fête de la Musique.

Toulouse's past and present coexist harmoniously, creating a dynamic city that preserves its heritage while embracing modernity. Its warm and welcoming atmosphere extends to everyone who visits, leaving a lasting impression and a desire to return.

As we conclude our Toulouse Travel Guide, we bid adieu to the Pink City with fond memories and the promise of future adventures. Whether you are a history enthusiast, a nature lover, a food connoisseur, or an art aficionado, Toulouse has something special to offer.

May your journey through the Pink City be filled with wonder, discovery, and joy. Until we meet again, bon voyage and vive Toulouse!

Printed in Great Britain
by Amazon

39369889R00069